Plan, Save, Buy

SOLD

A Simple Homebuying
Story with Phonics

Brandin Cureton

I0457106

Copyright © 2025 MG & B Publishing LLC
ISBN: 979-8-218-85972-5

All rights reserved. No part of this publication may be reproduced, distributed, or transmitted in any form or by any means, including photocopying, recording, or other electronic or mechanical methods, without the prior written permission of the publisher, except in the case of brief quotations embodied in reviews and certain other non-commercial uses permitted by the copyright law.

Published in the United States, an imprint of
MG & B Publishing LLC

Dedication

For every family with a big dream
and a small start.

And for every grown-up who never learned how
and they still want to.

This Book Belongs To:

_____

Dear Reader,

This book uses phonics because I believe in its power. Sounding out words is how I learned to read and comprehend the world around me. It gave me the confidence to keep going, even when the words felt big.

I hope that these pages feel simple, approachable, and encouraging for you, as well as for the children who read alongside you.

Like reading, buying a home is a process that happens one step at a time. I want this book to remind you that dreams are possible, and that you already possess what it takes to make them a reality.

With hope and belief in you,
Mr. Brandin, Your Real Estate Advisor

Affirmation

- I am ready to learn.
- I am ready to grow.
- I am ready to own a home, this much I know!

Let's Go

1

Hi! My name is Casey.
I am 8.
I love to plan.
I think it's great!

This is my Dad, Mr. Greg. He is smart. He is funny. He dreams BIG! He shows us the way, like a guiding light. He teaches us daily to do what is right. Standing next to Dad is my Mom, Ms. Sharon. She cares. She guides.

She helps us learn. She lights our way, showing that home is where hearts stay.

And this is my big brother, Miles. He is 11. He loves NUM-bers. (Say it with me: NUM-bers.) He counts for fun and solves small puzzles.

One day Dad said: "I am tired of rent.
I want a home! That's my intent."

I asked, "What does that mean?"

Miles said with cheer,
"It means we are the **land-lords**,
we make the rules for the land!"
(Land-lord. Say it with me: LAND-lord.)

We all smiled.
We all dreamed.
We all said: "Let's plan!"

Dad pulled out a note-book.
He said, "Casey, we need a plan."

Step 1: Plan
Step 2: Save
Step 3: Buy

Miles and I shouted:
"Yes! Let's do it!"

A plan is a map, a guide to the goal.
Step by step, we take control.

What's a Mortgage?

We learned that a house costs a LOT.
Too much to pay all at once.

Miles asked,
"How do we make the numbers make sense?"

Dad explained, "We borrow the money.
The bank calls that a **loan**."
(Loan. Say it with me: LOAN.)
But when a loan is for a house,
it has a special name.

It's called a **mortgage**.
(Mort-gage. Say it with me: MOR-gij.)
A mort-gage means:
Pay back a little each month for the house.

Month by month. Step by step.
We pay, we build, we do our part.

A mort-gage helps a dream to start.

Credit and Income

Mom explained,
"The bank won't just hand us money.
They need proof we're ready.
They want to see I have a job.
They want to see our **in-come**."
(In-come = the money you make.)

Then dad added,
"But the most important piece is **cred-it**.
Cred-it shows we can be trusted financially.
With good credit, the deal gets better."
(Cred-it. Say it with me: CRED-it.)

Save what you can, pay on time,
your credit will climb.

Saving Up

We saved, not spent.
Day by day.
Bit by bit.

Money from work.
Money from chores.
Every little saving
opens new doors.

Dad explained,
"This money we save at the start
is called a **down pay-ment**.
It's our very first part."

Save and save, both big and small,
the down payment helps us most of all.
(Down pay-ment = money we save first
to buy the house.)

Pre-approval Letter

We saved our money,
one dollar at a time.
Now came the moment
to see if we would qualify.

We went to a lender's website
to give it a try,
filled out the form—
click, tap, apply!

Then it came:
a **pre-approval letter.** Hooray!
Now we know the homes
that fit our budget for today

(Pre-ap-pro-val. Say it with me: pree-uh-PROO-vul.)

Getting Help

With our pre-approval in hand,
Dad called a **real es-tate agent**.
His name is **Mr. Brandin**.
A **real es-tate agent**
helps people buy and sell homes.

Mr. Brandin stepped in,
steady and smart.
"I'm more than an agent,
I serve from the heart."

"Our Real Estate Advisor!"
We said from the start.
He nodded, "Stick with me—
homefinding's my art."

Choosing the Right House

Some houses were too small.
Some were too far.

One had a foundation with a crack like
a scar.

But then, we saw it,
strong, safe, and bright.

"This is the one.
This home feels right."

The Offer

Dad said, "We're making an **offer**!"
(Off-fer. Say it with me: Off-fer.)

An offer means:
We tell the seller,
"We want to buy your home."

The seller can say yes.
The seller can say no.
Or the seller can say,
"Let's change the deal."

Home Inspection

Our offer was a YES!
Now came **due dil-i-gence.**
(**Due dil-i-gence** = time to check the house.)

An **in-spec-tor** walked inside and out.
(**In-spec-tor.** Say it with me: **IN-spec-tor.**)

He checked the roof. He checked the floor.
He peeked in windows. He opened each door.
"No leaks. No bugs. No cracks," he said.

We smiled and nodded.
We felt safe ahead.

Negotiations
(Ne-go-ti-ations)

We got the **in-spec-tion** report.
Some things were broken.
Some things were not.

Mom said, "We must ask the seller
to fix things."

So we said, "Please fix this.
Please fix that."

Back and forth. Yes and no.
Change a little. Let some go.

This back-and-forth is called **ne-go-ti-ating.**
(Ne-go-ti-ate. Say it slow: NE-go-shee-ate.)

26

Underwriting

This next step is called **un-der-writing.**
(Say it with me: UN-der-wri-ting.)

During this step, we met
the loan **pro-cess-or.**
(Say it with me: Praa-seh-sr.)

The pro-cess-or checks e-ver-y-thing:
Job. Cred-it. In-come.

They also ordered an **ap-prais-al.**
(Ap-prais-al = how much the
home is worth.)

Clear to Close

At last, the bank said the words:
"Clear to Close."

That means:
All papers are ready.
All forms are signed.
All checks are done.

Next stop, Closing Day!

Clear to close!
Soon, the keys will be ours to hold.

Closing Day

We went to a big office.
We signed LOTS of papers.
Dad said, "This is a **closing**."

Then... THE KEYS WERE OURS!

On Closing Day,
the wait was through.
The home was ours,
a dream come true.

Together we dreamed,
together we tried.
This home is our start,
our joy, our pride.

Dreams grow taller,
they stretch, they soar.
With hope in our hearts,
we'll reach for more!

Deed and Title

The **deed** is the paper that says,
"This is yours."
It names the new owner and
opens the doors.
(**Deed.** Say it with me: **DEED.**)

The **title** is proof, official and true.
It says, "This home belongs to you!"
(**Title.** Say it with me: **TY-tul.**)

DEED

This is yours.

Names the New Owner.
Opens the Doors!

TITLE

Proof, Official & True.
This Home Belongs to You!

Making It Ours

We painted the walls a bright, sunny hue.
We planted flowers that quickly grew.

We made our lists, both big and small.
At last, our home belonged to us all!

Step by step, with love and care,
we built a joy for all to share.

Why It Matters

Owning our home means:
We build E-qui-ty.
(Say it: ECK-wi-tee.
That means value we own.)

We can pass it down.
We can dream even BIGGER.
Home is where our plan became real.

The Plan Continues!

One day, I'll own two homes.

Miles planned to rent one of the homes out.

Mom wanted to learn about in-vest-ing.

Dad's next goal was fi-nan-cial free-dom.

Next Up in the Series:

"House Hack Heroes" – How to live for less and earn from your home

"Rent Like a Boss" – Becoming a landlord the smart way

"Fix It and Flip It" – Making money by improving homes

"Team Up and Buy Up" – Buying property with friends or family

Adult Corner:
Just the Basics

Mortgage: A loan from the bank to buy a home. You pay it back month by month.

Credit: Your record of paying bills on time. Good credit: better loan deals and lower interest rates.

Income: The money you make from your job. The bank checks this before lending.

Down Payment: The money you save first. It shows the bank you're serious.

Inspection: A professional check of the home to find problems.

Negotiation: The back-and-forth with the seller about repairs or price.

Underwriting: The bank's final review of your money, job, and credit.

Clear to Close: The bank says "yes." The loan is ready.

Closing Day: You sign the papers and receive the keys.

Choosing a mortgage

Types of Mortgages

When you borrow money to buy a home, you'll choose the type of mortgage that works best for your situation. Here are the most common ones:

FHA Loan*

- Backed by the government.
- Lower down payment (3.5%).
- Easier credit requirements.
- Great for first-time buyers.

VA Loan (For Veterans and Military Families)

- No down payment required.
- No private mortgage insurance (PMI).
- Must have military service history.

Conventional Loan

- Not backed by the government.
- Usually requires higher credit scores (620+).
- Down payment can be as low as 3% with good credit.
- May save money in the long run if you qualify.

USDA Loan (For Rural and Suburban Areas)

- No down payment.
- Lower mortgage insurance costs.
- Must buy in a qualified rural/suburban area.

*Most first-time buyers choose between FHA and Conventional loans. VA and USDA loans are amazing if you qualify.

What You Need to Qualify for an FHA Loan

- **Credit Score:** 620 or higher
- **Work History:** 2 years on the job or in the same field
- **Tax Returns**: 2 years of filed returns
- **Down Payment**: 3.5% of the purchase price
- **Extra Costs**: Moving expenses, home inspection, potential closing costs

⚠️ Note: These are common thresholds, but every lender might be slightly different.

FHA Loan FAQ

1. What if my credit score is below 620?
 Some lenders accept as low as 580, but you may face higher interest rates or extra conditions.

2. Do I need 2 years at the same job?
 Not always — lenders care more about stable, steady income in the same field.

3. Why are 2 years of tax returns required?
 They help prove your income is consistent and reliable.

4. How much is 3.5% down?
 On a $200,000 home, it's $7,000. Remember: you'll also need closing and moving costs.

5. What are closing costs?
 Fees for the loan, appraisal, title, and paperwork (usually 2%–5% of the purchase price).

6. Can I get help with the down payment or costs?
 Yes — through state/local programs, nonprofit grants, or family gifts.

7. Do I need perfect credit or finances?
 No. FHA loans are built for first-time buyers and those with less-than-perfect credit.

Plan, Save, Buy

Every story has an end—and a place to begin. You've learned the power of planning, saving, and stepping into homeownership. Now you know what it means to **Plan, Save, Buy.**

But your journey doesn't stop here. Dreams grow. Doors open. And with the right support, your next step is closer than you think. That's my promise:

From Dream to Home™

Scan the QR code for your **FREE** Homebuyer Checklist designed just for your journey.

Mr. Brandin, Your Real Estate Advisor

www.ingramcontent.com/pod-product-compliance
Lightning Source LLC
Chambersburg PA
CBHW041553120626
46551CB00002B/194